MODERN POLICE MOTORCYCLES
IN ACTION

ROBERT GENAT

MBI Publishing Company

First published in 1999 by MBI Publishing Company, 729 Prospect Avenue, PO Box 1, Osceola, WI 54020-0001 USA

MBI Publishing Company books are also available at discounts in bulk quantity for industrial or sales-promotional use. For details write to Special Sales Manager at Motorbooks International Wholesalers & Distributors, 729 Prospect Avenue, Osceola, WI 54020-0001 USA.

Library of Congress Cataloging-in-Publication Data
Genat, Robert.
    Modern police motorcycles in action/Robert Genat.
        p. cm.
    Includes index.
    ISBN 0-7603-0522-6 (pbk.: alk. paper)
    1. Police vehicles. 2. Motorcycles. 3. Traffic police.
I. Title.
HV7936.V4G46   1999
629.227'0883632—dc21   98-46893

On the front cover: In Europe, the BMW police motorcycle has been the standard for years. Today, it's challenging a market dominated by Kawasaki and Harley-Davidson.

On the frontispiece: The traditional winged wheel patch is worn with honor by police motorcycle officers. The same patch, without the wings, is worn by the members of a department's traffic division.

On the title page: For 90 years, freedom, adventure, and the chance to be part of an elite team has lured police officers onto the seats of police motorcycles. Being a motor officer is a fascinating and unpredictable line of work. It's also a lifestyle that these officers love.

On the back cover: (top) The Harley-Davidson FXRP is no longer in production, but the Salt Lake City Police Department has put a few of these reliable American motorcycles to good use. Like all Harleys, these police machines have a high resale value even after years of road wear. (bottom) You'd be smiling, too, if you were assigned to ride the hottest police motorcycle on the road today—the BMW R 1100 RT-P. The new Beemer offers eye-popping style and a host of advanced mechanical features, including ABS.

Edited by Christopher Batio

Designed by Todd Sauers

Printed in Hong Kong

CONTENTS

ACKNOWLEDGMENTS

It's unfortunate that most people only have the opportunity to meet a motor officer when they're getting a ticket. I can assure you, I have met them that way too! But in doing this project, I've been able to spend a lot of time with these officers without receiving a citation. What I found was a dedicated group of men and women who appreciate the long and proud heritage of the motor officer in America. They're real professionals who love their jobs and love riding motorcycles. Without their help and cooperation, I couldn't bring you this book. The following law enforcement agencies and officers went above and beyond the call of duty to help me with this project.

At the San Diego, California, Police Department, Chief Jerry Sanders, Assistant Chief John Welter, Motor Sergeants Todd Jarvis and Roger Higgins, and Motor Officers Chuck Shipler, Jim Dollins, Jim Bolen, Jay Odom, Joe Lopez, Jeff Pine, Terry Bennett, and Steve Burstein. Special thanks to Lieutenant Bill Brown.

At the California Highway Patrol, Commissioner Spike Helmick, Commander Kent Milton, Assistant Chief Fred Norton, Captain Dave Kissinger, Lieutenant Mike Alduenda, and State Traffic Officers Bill Grant, Micky Daley, Bob Schmeiser, Tony Herrera, Richard Hedgecock, Todd Wise, Jordan Ingels, and Michael Kennedy. Special thanks to State Traffic Officer Rick Sablan at the Oceanside CHP station.

At the Escondido, California, Police Department, Chief Duane White, Captain Lynn Nelson, and Motor Officer Don Shumate.

At the Carlsbad, California Police Department,

Officers Rob Shelton and Bruce May and Sergeant Bob Wick.

At the San Bernardino, California Sheriff's Department Emergency Vehicle Operations Center (EVOC), motorcycle instructors Steve Brinkerhoff, Bert Adkins, and Angelo Morgan.

At the San Diego County Sheriff's Department, Deputy Tim Petrachek.

At the Chula Vista, California, Police Department, Officers Eric Tarr and Kelly Harris.

At the Pontiac, Michigan, Police Department, Chief Larry McNeary.

My sincere thanks must also go out to the following motor officers: T. C. Hernandez, Rialto Police Department; Karl Murashima and Scott Sharpe, Cathedral City Police Department; Kevin Kirkman, Baldwin Park Police Department; Deputies Mike O'Brien, David Phelps, Troy McComas, Steve Geist, Greg Kreps, Wayne Martin, and Chris Allen, San Bernardino Sheriff's Department; John Lee, David Angarole, and Marv Griffin, Modesto Police Department; and Officer Michael Chard, Salt Lake City Police Department.

Thanks also to the manufacturers of the mighty machines featured in this book and their representatives: Frank Stevens, BMW of North America, Inc.; Jon Syverson, Harley-Davidson Motor Company, Inc.; and Henry Schnittker, Kawasaki Motors Corporation, U.S.A. Thanks to "Big" Bill Weisiger at Squad-Fitters and to Sonya Barnett at Kustom Signals. And finally, special thanks to photographers Michael Kan, James Genat, and Dale Stockton for the use of their excellent images.

—Robert Genat

INTRODUCTION

In the mid-1950s, my brother and I made regular trips to downtown Detroit to visit the orthodontist. We either caught the bus or were driven downtown by a relative, but the trip home was always on the bus. Our stop was directly adjacent to the Gaiety Burlesque House, which was a thrill in itself for a boy of 13. The other memorable part of our bus-catching experience was watching the activity at the Detroit Police Station across the street. It was there that I remember first seeing Harley-Davidson police motorcycles. I vividly recall watching the blue-suited officers rumbling away and reaching down to change gears with the tank-mounted shifter. I was so fascinated by those motorcycles that I proceeded to modify the three-speed handlebar shifter on my new Schwinn Corvette bicycle to look like one of those police Harleys. Unfortunately, my engineering skills at 13 couldn't solve the mechanical and safety problems I had created by placing the vertical shift lever on the crossbar. It never worked properly, but it was a cool concept.

When I moved to California in the early 1980s, I was exposed to the fabled California Highway Patrol (CHP). As a regular viewer of the *CHiPs* television series, I got the Hollywood version of police motorcycles. When my wife, Robin, and I researched our book, *Harley-Davidson Police Motorcycles*, I learned the true story about the men of the CHP and their machines. That research, along with my own limited motorcycle riding experiences, gave me a reasonably good foundation on which to start this project. I have also experienced that sinking feeling of looking in the rearview mirror to see the red and blue lights ignite on a big white motorcycle fairing. My last three tickets (all deserved) were courtesy of the CHP—two of them from motor officers. As a friend of mine recently said, "I haven't had a ticket in 15 years, but I deserve one every day!" Most of us do.

The spirit and tradition of the mounted rider lives on in today's police motorcycle officer. Along with much of the uniform, the independent spirit of the motor officer is similar to that of his counterpart on horseback.

The Machines— Hogs, Kawis, and Beemers

More than 100 years ago, bicycles were as common on the road as SUVs are today and were the vehicle of choice for the police officer on the beat. Bicycles, along with horses, allowed an officer to cover a much larger territory than he ever could on foot. Other than top speed, the bicycle offered several advantages over the horse. It never needed to be fed or cleaned up after, worked well on paved surfaces, and was highly maneuverable in tight spaces. Shortly after the turn of the century, the bicycle's top speed was overcome with the introduction of motor cars, and eventually, motorcycles. Even though early motorcycles were antiquated by today's standards, they brought an entirely new

If you just took a quick glance at the photo of these two Harley-Davidson police motorcycles, you might think it was taken in the 1960s. But, Harley-Davidson's timeless styling carries on today with the Road King model. *James J. Genat*

You can almost hear the distinctive rumble of this big Harley-Davidson V-twin engine. The fuel-injected 80-cubic-inch EVO engine thumps out a solid 83 foot-pounds of torque at 3,500 rpm. All Harley-Davidsons are equipped with an aramid fiber final belt drive. *James J. Genat*

The large white fairing on this Harley-Davidson identifies it as an Electra Glide model, Harley's premier police motorcycle. Unlike the Kawasaki and smaller Harley-Davidson FXRP, which have their fairing attached to the frame, the Electra Glide has its fairing attached to the front fork. *Michael Kan*

dimension to police work. Now the police officer had the agility of the bicycle and the speed of a motor vehicle, to keep up with those pesky new horseless carriages.

By the 1920s, the motorcycle was looking less like a bicycle with an engine and more like the motorcycle as we know it today. More powerful engines were added and multispeed transmissions became standard. In the 1930s, motorcycle manufacturers began to offer options, such as sirens and emergency lights, specifically for police use. Also in the 1930s, radios started to appear on police motorcycles. They were bulky, unreliable contraptions filled with fragile vacuum tubes, but they were the first step in coordinating all motorized police units.

By the mid-1950s, Harley-Davidson dominated the police motorcycle market. Indian had gone out of business, and foreign motorcycles were still seen as too frail and underpowered for America's roads. By the 1970s that would change, with many departments opting for Hondas, Suzukis, and Kawasakis. One manufacturer that became a major player in the police motorcycle arena in the 1970s was Moto Guzzi. The Los Angeles Police Department bought 10 to test and assigned them to what was known as the "Goose Patrol." The success of this experiment provided the encouragement for other major departments to also evaluate the Moto Guzzi.

In 1975, the California Highway Patrol's decision to purchase 130 Kawasakis gave its unofficial stamp of approval to the Japanese bike. At that time, the Kawasaki was the high-tech, high-performance champ, compared to the dated Harley-Davidsons. Within a few years, the Kawasaki was seen in action on the nationally broadcast television series, *CHiPs*. Ponch and John rode their CHP Kawasakis across southern California's roads from one daring law enforcement adventure to another. With all the high-profile visibility, Kawasaki was seen as *the* police motorcycle.

In 1981 Harley-Davidson redesigned itself and its police motorcycles. The shaky, unreliable machines of the past were once again becoming effective law enforcement machines. With the introduction in 1984 of the new EVO engine, with its familiar V-twin configuration, Harley was back on patrol. The folks at Harley-Davidson now had to face the formidable task of convincing departments that had switched to Kawasaki to ride Harleys again. Once again, the police motorcycle market was a solid two-horse race.

Today, history is repeating itself. The newest challenger on the police motorcycle block is Bavarian Motor Werks. BMW motorcycles have been the staple of European police departments for decades, and the German company is now trying to nudge its way into an American police motorcycle market dominated by Kawasaki and Harley-Davidson. Like

Each Harley-Davidson police motorcycle is equipped with a calibrated 120-mile-per-hour speedometer. Simplicity has always been a hallmark of Harley-Davidson design. *James J. Genat*

Kawasaki, BMW took on the most highly visible and toughest departmental nut to crack—the California Highway Patrol. An 80,000-mile test program was initiated in 1995 to evaluate the BMW. The CHP was impressed and placed an initial order for 150 machines. The new BMWs are radically different from any American police motorcycle in recent history. Will the officers who must ride them everyday accept these different machines, and will the agencies pay the high initial price? The first step is to compare the strengths and weaknesses of each make and model. Let's take a closer look at these motorcycles.

Harley-Davidson

The Harley-Davidson Motor Company has been serving the law enforcement community since 1908.

Sidecars are mounted on the right-hand side of these Harley-Davidson Electra Glides. Harley-Davidson is the only police motorcycle manufacturer to offer a sidecar for its motorcycles. Sidecars provide all-weather capability and are an asset when motoring slowly during a parade. *Michael Kan*

Harley-Davidsons were selected in the early days for their performance and dependability, the same reason they are selected today, more than 90 years later. Today the company supplies more than 1,000 law enforcement agencies in North America and 30 foreign countries. The legendary look and rumble of the V-twin is preserved in the three models designed specifically for police use. The engine and essential mechanicals on the Harley are virtually unchanged from the civilian version. All have the distinctive teardrop tank, a full-skirted front fender, and lots of chrome. Only the big bikes are offered today, all powered by the 1,340-cc (80 cid) Evolution OHV Vibration Isolated V-twin. The smaller FXRP Pursuit Glide is no longer manufactured but is still in service with many departments.

Motor officers who evaluated Harley-Davidson's revised Electra Glide as early as 1993 were astounded at the improvements to the machine, citing quick starting, good acceleration, comfortable suspension, sure-footed handling at high and low speed—all dramatic improvements over the Harley-Davidsons of the 1970s and early 1980s. Many officers feel the belt-drive system on the Harley-Davidson dramatically outperforms Kawasaki's chain drive.

The Harley-Davidson Motor Company worked steadily during the last decade to improve quality and match the performance and reliability of its competitors, while preserving those qualities that riders worldwide have found so irresistible—the sound, the look, and the feel of a Harley-Davidson. Officers who ride Harley-Davidsons often receive a friendly smile and thumbs-up from motorists along the road. Even an officer citing someone for a violation will occasionally be asked about his motorcycle and have the person receiving the ticket go back to admire the bike.

The FLHP Road King is Harley-Davidson's value-priced, entry-level police motorcycle. It has a standard powertrain with polished rocker boxes, timing cover, outer primary housing, and transmission covers. It also has a solo saddle that can be adjusted for comfort, using air pressure provided by a remote reservoir and monitored with a gauge. Water-resistant handlebar switches control all functions.

The Las Vegas Metro Police Department's motor officers have lined up their Harley-Davidsons in front of the Luxor Hotel. The first and third motorcycles in line are Electra Glides. The balance are the smaller framed FXRPs. *Las Vegas Metro Police Department*

The FLHPI Road King police motorcycle is equipped with electronic fuel injection and a 45-amp alternator. Its powertrain is finished in black with chrome engine trim. Both models sport a Lexan windshield with twin pursuit lights in a retro design that recalls the look of the 1950s and 1960s, before fairings became fashionable.

The legendary FLHTPI Electra Glide is Harley-Davidson's premier police motorcycle. It's identifiable by its fairing and windshield for all-weather protection. Features of the inner fairing include a microphone jack for a PA system, a pursuit light indicator, glove/radio box area, speaker pockets, and integral gauges.

13

The Harley-Davidson FXRP Pursuit Glide was last offered in 1994. It was built on the smaller Sportster frame, but featured the same EVO engine installed in the larger frame models. Many of these durable machines are still on patrol today.

The Harley-Davidson Road King is available with either a carburetor or a fuel-injected engine. Harley-Davidsons have the longest wheelbase and are the heaviest police motorcycles offered, features that result in an extremely smooth ride on the highway. *Dale Stockton*

All of the Harley-Davidson police models come equipped with a police-certified 120-mile per hour speedometer. On the rear are two large fiberglass saddlebags with police-type speed latches, which can be easily opened with one hand. The saddlebags are surrounded by sturdy chrome-plated guards. Up front, the engine guards are also chrome plated, and the adjustable floor boards are covered with nonskid rubber pads. The seat has an adjustable air suspension for an exceptionally comfortable ride.

Harley-Davidson also offers something the other manufacturers don't—a sidecar. In the 1920s and 1930s, sidecars were very popular with police departments. They provided an easy method of getting two officers to the scene of a crime quickly. Prior to the introduction of the three-wheeled Servi-Car, the sidecar also gave officers a low-speed platform needed for parking enforcement. Its greatest asset was the stability it gave the motorcycle in inclement weather. This is especially true in areas where police motorcycles are used year round, as they are in Washington, D.C. There, the National Capitol Area Park Police uses Harley-Davidsons equipped with sidecars for regular patrol and presidential escort, regardless of the weather.

Harley-Davidson's sidecar has a steel frame and a fiberglass body, with a fender that follows the same classic styling as the front fender on the motorcycle. The sidecar is attached to the frame of either the Road King or Electra Glide with several mechanical quick-disconnects. A plug-in electrical connector provides power for the sidecar's taillight, directional signal, and fender tip lamp. The interior of the sidecar is fully carpeted, including the lockable storage area behind the seat. The seat is comfortably padded and covered in vinyl. A contoured Lexan windshield protects the sidecar's passenger. Harley-Davidson provides a smart looking snap-down tonneau cover to protect the sidecar's passenger area when unoccupied.

Right
Kawasaki's police motorcycles have a faithful following among many law enforcement agencies across the country. Their low initial cost and ease of maintenance make them department favorites.

The officer on this motorcycle is about to shift into second gear. His left hand is about to squeeze the shift lever and the heel of his boot is poised to depress the shift lever for an up-shift.

highway, where the speed is relatively high and the big V-twin can effortlessly and smoothly thump along. The air suspension seat, longer wheelbase, and extra weight all add to the cruising enjoyment. At low speeds, the extra weight of the Harley-Davidson takes a little getting used to. But, also at low speeds, the long stroke of the engine provides plenty of torque for smooth handling. The one big intangible advantage over all other police motorcycles is the profound affection Americans have for the Harley-Davidson motorcycle.

Kawasaki

Manufactured in Lincoln, Nebraska, since 1976, the KZ1000 is still the mainstay of the two largest police motorcycle fleets in the United States—the California Highway Patrol and the Los Angeles Police Department—with hundreds of units in service.

One of the real keys to Harley-Davidson's success in the police market is the outstanding resale value of the motorcycles. The immense popularity of Harley-Davidson's street motorcycles, added to the collectablity factor of the police models, has kept resale values high.

Police officers riding Harley-Davidsons find them to be most comfortable on long stretches of

Kawasaki's overall penetration of the police market extends throughout America and to police and military organizations worldwide.

A proven workhorse for police officers, the KZ1000 has undergone only minor changes since 1982. This offers at least two major benefits to police departments. First, in-house maintenance managers enjoy the advantages of common parts, manuals, record-keeping, and service requirements. Next, repeat customers report motor officer training is easier and more efficient when only one brand of motorcycle is used. The addition of a new

Powering the Kawasaki KZ1000 is a dual-overhead cam in-line four-cylinder engine. Redline on this 92-horsepower engine is 8,500 rpm.

make to the fleet brings with it changes in turning, stopping, and handling characteristics. The operation runs more smoothly when one type of motorcycle is used exclusively.

The basic layout and configuration of the KZ1000 have remained the same since it was introduced in the 1970s. It comes standard with a frame-mounted fairing, sturdy Lexan windshield, disc brakes front and rear, large solo seat, and specially dampened radio rack. An example of a recent product improvement is a change to the type of finish used on the frame. The new finish is more durable

Kawasaki police motorcycles are equally at home on city streets or on the freeway. Their short (60.4-inch) wheelbase allows them to easily weave through congested downtown traffic, and their swift acceleration allows them to quickly chase down highway speeders.

Reliability is high on the list of what motor officers want in a motorcycle. The Kawasaki KZ1000 has millions of road-proven miles with departments worldwide.

and more aesthetically appealing. Another recent feature is the sidestand ignition lockout that prevents the motorcycle from being started with the sidestand in its down position. Routine service intervals are scheduled every 3,000 miles—just like most of today's passenger cars—and the motorcycle comes with a 12-month, unlimited mileage warranty.

Sergeant Todd Jarvis rides a Kawasaki KZ1000 for the San Diego, California, Police Department. He also owns a 1997 Harley-Davidson Heritage Soft Tail. "When I'm on the Kawasaki, it's for work and when I'm on the Harley, it's all for fun," says Jarvis with a smile. Recently, after a full day of patrolling the streets on his Kawasaki, Jarvis hopped on his Harley-Davidson to visit a friend. "The Harley brings a smile to my face. It's so comfortable and loud."

Jarvis didn't feel he could make a fair comparison of the Harley-Davidson and the Kawasaki, having not ridden the Harley-Davidson for law enforcement.

"I haven't really tried to get my Harley into the tight turns and things we do with the Kawasaki," says Jarvis. "I really don't think it would handle as well in some of the tight situations we get into, such as jumping curbs. I've taken that Kawasaki some amazing places, like chasing people down stairwells. It just goes! I don't think the Harley could do that. But then again, I haven't really taken my Harley out and ridden it in the same way as I have the Kawasaki, because the Harley is *mine*."

Without a doubt, the Kawasaki KZ1000 police motorcycle is a workhorse of the roads. It has proven itself time and time again to be an excellent law enforcement motorcycle. The Kawasaki has the tightest turning radius of any police motorcycle, which allows it to weave smoothly through traffic snarls and city congestion. The Kawasaki also is the acceleration leader of the group. Acceleration is a key element in catching speeders, and the Kawasaki's 80-horsepower engine winds up quickly and smoothly. The KZ1000's reliability is another factor police officers appreciate. Currently, it's not unusual for a Kawasaki to rack up 70,000 to 80,000 miles of service—110,000 is the record.

Every Kawasaki police motorcycle comes standard with a fiberglass fairing, pursuit lights, saddlebags, and large saddle style seat. Its heavy-duty electrical system is designed for the extra load placed on it by the radio and emergency lights.

Still, Kawasaki admits that the KZ1000 has seen its better days. Motorcycle technology has marched on while the KZ1000 has stood still. While there are many motor officers who like the current model, Kawasaki is going ahead with plans for an all-new police motorcycle. Scheduled for a 1999 or 2000 release, the new bike will be based on Kawasaki's Nomad model, a V-twin cruiser that resembles a Harley-Davidson and features a liquid-cooled 1,500-cc engine and shaft drive. Henry Schnittker, Kawasaki's senior manager of police, military, and government sales, admits that not all of the design features for the new police motorcycle have been locked in. Under discussion are antilock brakes, the design of the windshield and fairing, and adding an adjustable seat and saddlebags.

"When we come out with the new model," says Schnittker, "We will continue with the current KZ1000 model for at least two years. There's a strong following of people who like it, and we have

Off-Road Police Motorcycles

Not all police motorcycles patrol the highways. Some are assigned to patrol areas that would not be friendly to a Harley-Davidson, Kawasaki, or BMW. Theses areas are the undeveloped regions and parks that exist in many large cities and counties. Many of these areas have hiking trails and campsites that cannot easily be accessed by four-wheel-drive vehicles.

The machines used by many law enforcement agencies are standard off-road motorcycles powered by engines with up to 600 cc. A few types are specially modified by the manufacturer for off-road police work and are outfitted with lights and sirens similar to those on street patrol motorcycles.

The mission of the off-road motorcycle is to carry law enforcement into areas where the terrain is too rough for any other kind of police vehicle. In remote recreational areas that are used by ATVs and mountain bikers, an off-road motorcycle may be the only way a department can do its job. Off-road motorcycles are used extensively by the U.S. Border Patrol to monitor the southern border of the United States, to patrol remote areas used by drug smugglers, and to apprehend undocumented foreign nationals. The southern border area contains many empty acres where migrant or transient encampments may need to be monitored. During fires in remote wilderness areas, the off-road motorcycle can be used to help notify and evacuate stranded homeowners or to help direct fire fighting efforts.

The officers riding these motorcycles may or may not be part of their department's motor unit, but they are given special training that focuses on safety. Much of the protective equipment these officers wear is the same type that any recreational off-road rider might wear. Officers also carry a standard service weapon, along with extra magazines, mace and handcuffs. The duty belt worn is usually made of nylon instead of leather.

Not all police motorcycles patrol the streets. These two ATK off-road bikes are specially modified for law enforcement work in remote areas. The officers usually ride in pairs. They wear commercially available off-road protection equipment, in addition to their police gear. *Dale Stockton*

departments with a store of spare parts. Some police departments have budgets that are based on the KZ1000 and there are a lot of department mechanics who are trained on it, too."

BMW

Look out, Harley-Davidson and Kawasaki—there's a new kid on the block. In some neighborhoods, BMW stands for "Break My Windows," but today, BMW stands for a new police motorcycle that's been creating a stir in departments all across the country.

BMW has been serving the police vehicle market worldwide for decades. Today, police agencies in more than 120 foreign countries ride the BMW motorcycle. Although, it's only within the past few years that BMW has invaded the U.S. police

motorcycle market, where its presence is growing at a fast rate.

The California Highway Patrol recently concluded a long-term evaluation of 10 BMW K75 RT-Ps. Not long after the evaluation started, BMW discontinued this 750-cc–powered in-line three-cylinder model and replaced it with the much different 1,085-cc flat twin. The motorcycles were used in routine traffic patrol throughout the state of California. This thorough evaluation looked at performance, high- and low-speed handling, reliability, durability, safety, rider response to the vehicle, and adaptability to the real world of police work.

According to BMW's Fleet Sales Manager, the BMW R1100 RT-P (P for police) offers the advanced technology and engineering of the 1990s to its police customers. Offered for the first time

Peeking out from behind this new California Highway Patrol BMW R 1100 RT-P is the motorcycle it will be replacing, the Kawasaki KZ1000. Late in 1997, the CHP signed a contract for 150 BMW motorcycles. The CHP's service life of these motorcycles is three years or 60,000 miles.

The BMW's cross-drilled 12-inch-diameter front brake rotors look as though they came off a Grand Prix race car. BMW comes standard with cross-spoke 3.5x18-inch wheels fitted with 110/80 ZR 18 tires. Cast alloy wheels are optional. The gear-like ring on the inside of the rotor is the trigger wheel for the front wheel ABS. There is a similar trigger wheel on the rear axle. BMW's ABS is a first for police motorcycles.

on a police motorcycle is BMW's ABS (antilock braking system) which operates independently on both the front and rear wheels. The rider's seat offers three height adjustments and the windshield's rake is electrically adjustable. The shift lever is adjustable to two different heights and the front brake lever can be adjusted to four different positions. There are adjustable hot air vents for the rider's hands and BMW even offers optional heated handlebar grips. The 90-horsepower opposed-twin engine is air-oil cooled by means of a thermostatically controlled oil cooler and auxiliary cooling fans. This allows the motorcycle to idle for long periods while keeping its temperature down. A high-output alternator (50 amps) provides plenty of

power for radio, lights, and sirens. BMW's special police package also includes an auxiliary battery for reserve power.

The advanced technology and engineering of the BMW comes at a cost. The price tag on the R 1100 RT-P is higher than that of its competitors, but BMW executives believe the bike offers inherent value worth this additional cost. They also believe that, in the long term, these bikes will work reliably for longer periods of time, and that the cost will spread out over the life of the motorcycle.

One significant difference between the BMW and its two rivals is the drive system. The BMW's shaft drive is cheaper to maintain and more reliable than Kawasaki's chain drive, but requires slightly more maintenance than the Harley's belt drive. However, a trade-off is increased torque reaction when rolling on and off the throttle. In a traditional shaft drive, this transmits a "pogo" effect to the rider—a rising and falling of the rear end. BMW engineers have minimized this torque effect by having the alternator and other accessories to spin in the opposite direction to the shaft. They also designed a unique paralever rear end to counteract the "pogo" effect.

Intended for an international market, the European style of the R 1100 RT-P results in a riding position quite different from what most American police motor officers are used to. Foot placement, seat location, and handlebar configuration tend to place the rider in a slightly forward-leaning position. This transfers more of the rider's weight to the hands and wrists at low speed. However, the design has its advantages at high speeds, where airflow supports the rider leaning into it, thereby lifting weight off the hands.

The new BMW police motorcycle looks nothing like any other production police motorcycle sold in the United States. Inside the two nostrils below the headlight is the oil cooler. The BMW has an auxiliary fan to draw air through the oil cooler if the motorcycle must be parked with the engine running for an extended period.

Police Motorcycles at a Glance

	BMW, R 1100 RT-P	Harley-Davidson, FLHP	Kawasaki, KZ1000
Price (approx.)	$15,990	$14,000	$7,500
Wheelbase	58.3 inches	62.9 inches	60.4 inches
Curb weight	622 pounds	712 pounds	595 pounds
Fuel capacity	6.8 gallons	5 gallons	4 gallons
Engine	2-cylinder opposed	2-cylinder V-twin	4-cylinder in-line
Displacement	1,085 cc	1,340 cc	998 cc
Horsepower	90	72	92
Gearbox	5-speed	5-speed	5-speed
Drive	Shaft	Belt	Chain
Cooling system	Air/oil	Air	Air
Brakes	Antilock disc	Disc	Disc
Top speed (mph)	120	103	107
Quarter-mile	97 mph in 13.28 sec	88 mph in 14.53 sec	96 mph in 13.11 sec
Service intervals	6,000 miles	3,000 miles	3,000 miles
Est. resale value	$6,500	$12,000–$15,000	$800–$1,500

The R 1100 RT-P rider position has one distinct disadvantage for its police riders—interaction between the spit-shined boots of a motor officer and the shifter. On Harley-Davidsons and Kawasakis, the officer's left foot rests on a floor board and up-shifts are done with the heel pushing down on the shift lever. This preserves the shine on the toe of the motor officer's polished boot, however, there are no floorboards on the R 1100 RT-P, only foot pegs. It shifts like a conventional street bike, where the rider uses the top of his or her toe to push the shift lever up for shifting. Several first-time riders said they noticed a more distinctive mechanical snap when shifting the BMW, compared to the Kawasaki.

The BMW is a smooth-riding machine with excellent handling. Some are concerned that, because the BMWs are so smooth, officers may ride them faster than usual. After riding a BMW for two weeks, veteran CHP Motor Officer Bob Schmeiser commented on how well the BMW was balanced and how smooth it was. He also remarked on how well it cornered at speed. "I have only one complaint. It's too quiet." Schmeiser laughingly suggested a method he once used to get a more mellow exhaust tone out of the Harley-Davidsons he rode. "We used to stick a metal rod up through the muffler to knock out the baffles!"

One immense advantage of the BMW over the Harley-Davidson and Kawasaki is ABS. This braking system allows the BMW to come to a smooth, safe stop from any speed, without a skid. The front and rear ABS work independently of each other. When testing a new BMW for the first time, a CHP officer came to a smooth stop from 50 miles an hour using only the rear brake. "I had it jammed as hard as I could," he said, referring to the right foot pedal that controls the rear brake. Attempting this on any non-ABS bike would result in a rear-wheel skid and likely fall. This officer's only concern was the potential danger of getting comfortable with the ABS brakes and then switching back to a bike without ABS. But he supports the use of ABS in rainy weather. There have been several nights when this officer had to ride home in the rain very carefully on his Kawasaki. He feels the BMW's ABS brakes would be a great benefit in such foul weather situations.

The BMW's sleek mirror housings (which also incorporate the amber turn signals) are a break-away design. The engine guards on this BMW are used to mount a radar antenna and the siren speaker.

In addition to a seat that adjusts to three heights, the BMW has a windshield with an adjustable rake. While on the road, the officer can electronically adjust it with the touch of a button.

Powering the BMW police motorcycle is a two-cylinder opposed engine that produces 90 horsepower. Each cylinder has four valves, and the engine has a total displacement of 1,085 cc. The officer riding the BMW must rest his feet on foot pegs, because traditional police motorcycle floorboards are not part of the package.

Performance, durability, reliability, comfort, and safety—these are the things motor officers look for when choosing motorcycles for police work. The bean counters in the accounting department want a motorcycle with a low initial purchase price, low maintenance costs, a good warranty program, and a favorable resale value. And everyone in the department wants a motor that looks good. The trick for any department is to identify a motorcycle that meets all of these requirements.

Law enforcement now has three major players to look at, with each offering a distinct product. All of these motorcycles are solid platforms for police work. All have proven themselves worldwide over many years. If you were a police officer, which one would you ride? As one dedicated motor officer chuckled, "You can get used to anything, when the alternative is four wheels."

The instrument panel of the new BMW is just as attractive as the external styling. Air ducts direct warm air to the rider's hands. For that extra toasty feeling, optional heated handgrips are available. The green switch on the left handgrip controls the rake of the windshield. The yellow switch on the right handgrip activates the emergency lights.

2

Special Equipment— Lasers and Leather

Outfitting the Motorcycle

Each police motorcycle is designed to carry the equipment necessary for law enforcement. Some of the equipment is for the safety of the officer, and some is to help the officer do the job. No matter the make or model of the motorcycle, they are all equipped the same.

Being a police motorcycle officer requires skill and experience to ride safely. Both the motorcycle and the officer require special equipment to do the job effectively. Sergeant Todd Jarvis is typical of today's highly skilled motor officer. He rides a Kawasaki KZ1000 and proudly wears the uniform of the San Diego, California, Police Department.

Saddlebags

Each police motorcycle has a pair of saddlebags, located on either side of the rear wheel. The first saddlebags used on police motorcycles were made of leather and were very similar to those used on horses. Today they are made of plastic or fiberglass and can hold an amazing amount of equipment. One side is typically used for the items required by the department and the other side is used for personal articles.

A motor officer usually carries a copy of the vehicle code book. This book lists all the state violation codes (laws) that the officer is responsible for enforcing. This book is large, and it takes up quite a bit of space. (California's 1,500-page code book is 1.8 inches thick.) Also carried are a spare ticket book, a small first aid kit, and a local map. Most officers also carry rags to wipe down their motorcycle. Kawasaki riders carry chain oil. If the motorcycle is outfitted with a radar or laser unit, the "pigtails" for the electrical connection will also be stored in the saddlebags. A small supply of road flares is also kept in the saddlebags. Some officers carry a small tool kit to make quick roadside repairs. Latex gloves are also now becoming standard equipment for any officer who works the streets, and these will be found in the saddlebags.

If the officer knows that there may be some time spent at one of the department's posts, he might carry

The saddlebags on the Harley-Davidson Road King (pictured) and Electra Glide have a stylish forward rake. They are protected by a set of chrome bars. Attached to the rear of the motorcycle is a rotating beacon at the end of an adjustable pole.
James J. Genat

a regulation uniform hat in the saddlebags. Motor officers often start the day wearing a jacket in the cool of the morning. As the day warms, the jacket is placed in one of the saddlebags. An officer might also carry bottles of drinking water, snacks, and sometimes a brown bag lunch. While working traffic at the local sports stadium, one officer carries a portable AM/FM radio so he will know when the game was about to end. Another motor officer says he carries a personal tape recorder to tape traffic stops. On

Left
The saddlebags on this Kawasaki provide storage for a host of law enforcement equipment and the officer's personal belongings. One thing you will always find in the saddlebags of a police motorcycle is a rag to wipe down the motorcycle.

more than one occasion he has used the tape in court, much to the embarrassment of the defendant.

Radar and Laser
As police officers charged with enforcing the traffic code, motorcycle officers target speed violators. Hand-held radar and laser units, used for detecting speed, are excellent law enforcement tools. While similar in outward appearance, these units use different technologies to track speed.

Radar has been an effective traffic enforcement tool for many years. It works just like the radar used in aircraft. A radio frequency pulse is sent out by the unit. This wave of radio energy hits an object and returns as an echo that the system receives. The system calculates the elapsed time between pulses and displays the speed. The type of radar used for traffic enforcement is K-Band Doppler, which has an operating frequency of 24.15 GHz. The laser units work on the same basic principle, measuring a vehicle's speed based on the return signal that bounces off of it. The only difference is a laser beam is aimed at the car, instead of radio waves.

Radar and laser units each have advantages and disadvantages. The radar units, with their broader beam width, cover a larger area and do not need to be aimed as precisely as the laser guns. But this can also be a disadvantage since the radar gun cannot discriminate targets on a busy street. On a congested highway, the unit may receive echoes from several targets and the readings might not be accurate. Radar works best where there is a limited amount of traffic and the system can easily track a single target. Hand-held radar and laser guns weigh slightly over three pounds each.

Laser guns must be brought up to the user's eye and a cross hairs in the eyepiece must be held on a vehicle in order for the unit to get a good lock on the target. The laser emits a small beam, only 4 feet wide at 1,000 feet. Within the eyepiece is a heads-up display that reveals the target vehicle's speed and range. Once the system has detected the speed, the gun will emit an electronic beep. The speed can then be read on a digital display at the back of the gun. Because the laser must be brought up to the user's eye, it limits the officer's peripheral vision, preventing him from noticing any other traffic violators in the area. Because laser guns are aimed at one specific vehicle, they are extremely effective in congested areas. Laser guns that display range information are also used to take quick measurements for accident investigations.

The most frequently used technique for either hand-held laser or radar guns is for the motor officer to park off to the side of the road. The officer will park facing out among a row of parked cars or on a side street, usually in the shade. The shade is one of the most important factors because sitting in the sun with a helmet and body armor on can become very uncomfortable. It's much easier to catch a speeder coming at you than one going away from you, so that's the way motor officers run their radar. With a car coming at the officer holding the radar gun, the system will read and

display the vehicle's speed. The officer has enough time to put the radar gun away, start the motorcycle, and roll out into traffic behind the speeder.

Both laser and radar guns are small enough to be stored on any police motorcycle. They are most commonly found on the top of, or in front of, one of the saddlebags. The holders, commonly called holsters, for these units can be commercially purchased, but are often made by the department's mechanics.

All officers who use radar or laser guns must be certified in their use. Officers attend a three-week certification class. Here, they learn how to visually estimate a vehicle's speed and proper techniques for use of the laser and radar. They also learn how to calibrate the radar guns. Some motor officers calibrate their radar every day, because the first question asked when in court for a radar stop is, "When was the last time your radar was calibrated?"

Also found on police motorcycles are holders for the officer's baton (nightstick) and flashlight. Some police motorcycles are also being equipped with shotguns. Mounted in the saddlebag area, bracketry for the shotgun is similar to the electro-mechanical lock mounts found in patrol cars.

Fairings

Motorcycle fairings came into vogue in the mid-1970s. Many officers resisted, feeling that the fairings upset the high-speed handling. Today they are standard equipment, with the exception of certain Harley-Davidson models. Made of fiberglass, fairings deflect the wind around the officer, serve as a mount for the windshield, and provide a convenient location for the forward-facing pursuit lights. On the inside of the fairing are small compartments, where the officer can store an extra pair of gloves or other small personal items. For easy access, most officers keep their ticket book tucked somewhere on the inside of the fairing.

Typically, pursuit lights mounted on the fairing are a combination of red and blue, the two colors we associate most with police emergency lights. Studies have shown that the red lights are more effective during the daytime and the blue lights are more effective at night. The use of additional emergency lights on the

The Kawasaki KZ1000 comes standard with a fairing that is attached to the frame. It houses two emergency pursuit lights. On this motorcycle, the red light is halogen and the blue light is a strobe.

rear and side of the motorcycle varies greatly among departments. Some attach a pole-mounted rotating red or blue beacon, or strobe, off the rear of one of the saddlebags. These are usually found on Harley-Davidsons and BMWs. Red and blue lights can also be found on the rear and sides of the radio box. The motorcycle's emergency lights are either halogen or strobes, but a full complement of strobes is becoming very popular on police motorcycles. On January 1, 1978, all on-road motorcycles were required to have a headlight that would illuminate as soon as the motorcycle's engine started. Police motorcycles are exempt from this law and have a switch for the headlight. Even though it's legal for police motorcycles to run in the daytime without a headlight, many officers prefer to leave them on.

Sirens

The first sirens used on police motorcycles were the "growler" type. This type of siren was mechanical, driven by one of the rotating tires. To engage the siren, the officer depressed his heel against a lever that would swing the siren's knurled armature into contact with the rear tire. This would get the siren up to full screeching song. On some police motorcycles, this type of siren was also mounted on the front fender and was brought into contact with the front tire with the use of a lever on the handlebars. At high speeds, these sirens would spin so fast that they would often explode or, in the winter, they would often freeze solid and not spin at all. The screech of these sirens was so deafening that no one was upset when they were replaced with the electronic siren.

With the push of a button on the handlebars, the familiar electronic yelps and wails of the patrol car are duplicated on today's police motorcycles. Mounted on the front engine guard, the siren's 100-watt speaker faces forward. An electronic amplifier in the radio box provides the power. The siren speakers

33

can also be also used as a public address system, either through the officer's helmet-mounted microphone or a hand-held microphone.

Radios

In the early days of police motorcycles, there was no way for headquarters to directly communicate with the officers while they were on the road. Motor officers would call in to the precinct at predetermined intervals. If the department needed an officer quickly, they would telephone a business along the officer's beat and that business would hang a red flag on its store front. This flag indicated to the officer that something was going on that he or she needed to know about. The officer would then stop and call headquarters using the phone at the business displaying the red flag.

The first police radios on motorcycles were seen in the early 1930s. These low-power AM-band radios, controlled by fragile vacuum tubes, could only receive signals and were very unreliable. To get enough voltage to operate the radio, the officer often had to rev the motorcycle's engine and put an ear down on the speaker to hear what was being broadcast. In 1941, California Highway Patrol radio technician Ray Burton developed the first practical

A fairing is standard equipment on the Harley-Davidson Electra Glide. This Michigan State Police unit is painted in the department's traditional blue paint scheme. All emergency lights on this motorcycle are red, another Michigan State Police tradition. If you look closely, you will notice that this trooper is wearing a necktie. For safety, it's a clip-on. *Michael Kan*

two-way radio for motorcycles. Even though it lacked power, it gave the motor officer two-way communication with a dispatcher.

In June 1957, Motorola introduced the "Dispatcher Radiophone." It represented a significant design change in police radios. No longer an adaptation of an automobile unit, this radio was designed specifically for police motorcycles. It was a smaller package that featured transistors, replacing the vacuum tubes of the older designs. Power consumption was now down to 1 amp to receive and 15 amps to transmit. The next significant improvement in radios for police motorcycles was the jump to a 12-volt electrical system in the mid-1960s.

Today's police radios are smaller, lighter and more powerful than ever. They have multichannel capability and include scanners, which allow the officer to monitor neighboring communities and highway patrol units for mutual aid situations. Today's radios also have the ability to select a primary channel while scanning several secondary channels. Even though the radio technology is better than ever, it's still difficult to hear radio calls when traveling down the highway. Most motor officers listen only to their primary channel to avoid the confusion of hearing multiple calls on their headsets.

Even the smallest police departments have at least two frequencies for broadcasts. The primary frequency is reserved for everyday radio calls. The second frequency is considered a tactical frequency and is reserved for situations where a clear radio channel is important, such as during an extended vehicle pursuit. The tactical channel gives those involved their own clear channel on which to broadcast. The primary channel continues to broadcast regular radio calls to all other units not involved in the pursuit. These other units are able to scan the tactical channel to follow the developing situation. Within larger departments, certain specialized departmental functions (SWAT, Investigation, Traffic Control, and Surveillance) have their own discreet frequencies.

Police radio frequencies are all carried within four bands, VHF-low (30.000–50.000 MHz), VHF-high (138.000–174.000 MHz), UHF (470.000–

Hand-held laser units must be brought up to the user's eye and aimed at a specific vehicle. This Kustom Signals Pro-Laser II has a heads-up display that verifies the target and the target's speed. When the crosshairs are close to a moving target, the unit emits an intermittent tone. Once locked on, the tone becomes continuous. The range of this laser gun is over 2,000 feet.

512.000 MHz), and 800 MHz (806.000–940.000 MHz). A quick glance at the motorcycle's radio antenna is an easy way to determine the frequency on which that particular department communicates. A VHF-low antenna will be the longest, with a 35-inch whip with a 5-inch coil at the bottom. The VHF-high will have an 18-inch whip. UHF will have either a 6-inch whip or a 32-inch whip with a 3-inch coil in the middle. Many departments are moving into radio systems that broadcast on the 800 MHz band; these are the easiest to identify with their stubby 3-inch antennas.

The days of the motor officer grabbing a hand microphone to make a radio call while in pursuit are long gone. Fitted inside the helmet are a pair of earphones and a boom microphone for the radio. A simple push of a button on the handlebars

35

The officer seated on this Harley-Davidson Road King is running his cordless radar unit while parked along a coastal route. He's backed into the curb at a 90-degree angle to the traffic flow. From this position, he can track oncoming traffic from either direction. *Dale Stockton*

allows the motor officer to communicate. This simple technology allows the motor officer to keep both hands on the control grips at all times, a big safety factor when chasing a bad guy down the road, transmitting the location and describing the vehicle.

Outfitting the Officer

Motor officers are the most highly visible law enforcement personnel in any department, and they're part of a lengthy history of mounted officers that reaches back well into the 1800s. The honor and tradition of the motor officer is kept alive by today's riders. Part of that tradition is preserved in the unique uniform motor officers wear and the way it's maintained. The uniform's history of breeches and high boots is rooted in the same uniform worn by officers mounted on horseback. This uniform was adapted by early motor officers and continues with little change today.

Appearance is an important part of being a motor officer. There's an undeniable "cool" to patrolling the roads on two wheels, and the officers who ride these motorcycles love it. Part of the motor officer tradition is always looking sharp, and that applies to both the motorcycle and the officer's personal appearance. A motor officer's uniform is always military crisp. Great pride is taken in the shine of their high top boots and the metallic components of their uniforms.

Boots

The motor officer wears high top boots for protection and tradition. When a motorcycle goes down into a slide, the first part of the officer's body likely to meet the pavement are the feet, legs, and ankles. Because of the way the ankle bone protrudes, it is particularly vulnerable during a slide. The thick leather on the boot offers protection to

A hand-held radar gun weighs a little over three pounds. This particular unit draws its power from the motorcycle's battery. On this cool morning, this officer has donned his leather jacket and well-worn gauntlet-style gloves.

that vulnerable area. The high gloss on a motor officer's boots is a product of a military-style spit shine. The prices for these boots range from $300 for standard, off-the-shelf sizes to $600 for a custom-made pair. Boots can last as long as three years, but rain and road debris eventually take their toll on the leather. It also takes about three years for the "stacks to fall." The "stack" is the upper portion of the boot. When the area around the ankle starts to get too soft, the stack will slide down, causing unsightly wrinkles at the ankles.

Most officers prefer thick soles on their boots and will often place metal taps on the heels. The taps echo distinctively when a motor officer walks down the marble hallways of a courthouse, and they produce spectacular rooster tails of sparks when they're dragged along the pavement at night. The motor officer also clips a writing pen or a small flashlight on the inside top edge of his or her boot, and some officers also carry a concealed knife there.

Breeches

Tucked neatly into those high-top boots are the officer's breeches. They're not called pants or trousers—they're breeches! They fit snugly and are reinforced in the seat for wear. Fabrics vary from 100 percent wool to blends of cotton, nylon, polyester, and Lycra. The types of material and percentages of the blend vary with the season and departmental uniform selection. Some officers still wear the jodhpur-style riding breech that is cut full through the hips.

Shirt

The motor officer's uniform shirt is standard issue—short sleeves for summer and long sleeves for winter. The material and fabric blends closely follow those of the breeches. Many departments allow their motor officers to wear turtleneck sweaters under their jackets in the winter. On colder days, motor officers often wear thermal underwear. One motor officer told me— anonymously—that to keep warm, he and a few other male officers wear women's panty hose under the breeches—a cold weather innovation originated by professional football players.

Body Armor

Since Kevlar was introduced by Du Pont in the early 1970s, body armor has saved the lives of more than 2,000 law enforcement officers. Today, virtually all police officers working the streets wear a protective vest (soft body armor) of some kind. There are a multitude of body armor styles and protection levels for patrol officers to chose from. Vests are designed to protect the front and back torso. Most are made of Kevlar, which is woven into a fabric and designed to dissipate impact energy throughout the weave of the vest. Kevlar is five times stronger than an equal weight of steel. When struck by a bullet, its fibers absorb and disperse the impact energy to surrounding fibers in the weave of the fabric. Kevlar vests also may protect a rider in an accident, and they have been shown to be effective against slashing knife attacks, club attacks, and even explosions. One officer told me of being struck in the chest with a 2-by-4 during a confrontation with a young man resisting arrest. Without the vest, he would probably have had several

Today, all police motorcycle sirens are electronic. What is attached to the front engine guard is a speaker for 100 watts of electronic yelps and wails. The speaker can also be used as a public address loud speaker. *James Genat*

broken ribs, but the blow didn't even knock the wind out of him. The thug was stunned when the officer wasn't fazed by the blow. With a big smile the officer said, "It's almost like being Superman in a fight."

Other synthetic materials used for protective vests are Araflex and Twaron, which both have the same basic characteristics as Kevlar. One of the newest materials being used in protective vests is Ceramicized Glass Armor, also known as CGA. This material is fabricated from woven glass fibers and laminated with thermoactive resins. When a vest with CGA is struck by a bullet, its surface sheds its laminated layers in sequence, which decreases the projectile's speed and deforms it.

Various types and styles of protective vests are offered to law enforcement officers. Each officer must assess the threat he or she expects to encounter on the road and determine the amount of body coverage required. Different levels of protection will determine how thick the vest should be and how much it will weigh, commonly ranging from 2 to 5 pounds. The amount of protection can be enhanced with panels that cover the sides of the upper body, but they add to the weight of the vest and increase retention of body heat. Added heat is the price paid for wearing a protective vest, since they do not breathe and can be very uncomfortable, especially on a hot, humid day. It's not unusual for an officer to wear one

The control head, speaker, microphone, and helmet jack for the radio is mounted directly in front of the officer. The hand microphone is used when the officer's helmet jack is unplugged or if the electronics fail.

or two T-shirts under the vest to absorb excessive perspiration. Ribbed and open-mesh T-shirts are also used to help improve circulation under the vest. Body armor costs from $200 to $600, a small price to pay for lifesaving protection. Because the protective vest is a safety item, most departments provide them for their officers. The departments also replace them on a regular schedule and, of course, if they are damaged in the line of duty.

Helmets

All police motor officers wear helmets while on the road. Motor officers wear three basic styles of helmets, the half-shell, the three-quarter shell, and the full-face helmet. The half-shell helmet protects only the area of the skull above the ears. These are the original police helmets, first seen in the 1950s. The other helmet used by motor officers is the three-quarter shell type. This style features an open-face design,

All police officers stay in contact with the dispatcher by means of radio communication. This BMW has its radio mounted in the white box behind the rider's seat. The pigtail for the helmet microphone and headset is plugged into the radio control head. This officer carries a portable radio that broadcasts on the same frequency as the one on his motorcycle. Some motorcycle officers carry only a portable radio.

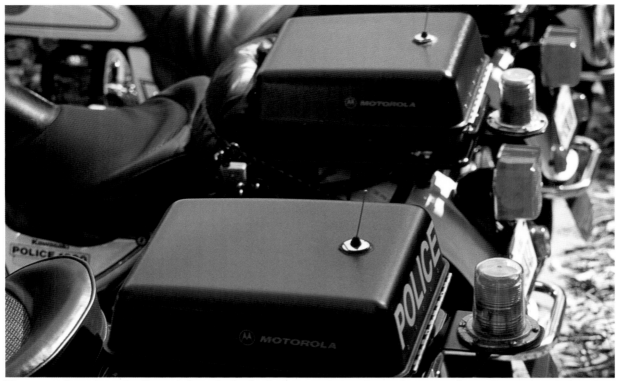

The rear radio rack on the Kawasaki has a hydraulic dampener, which is designed to rotate from side to side to help reduce oscillations of the motorcycle. The stubby 3-inch whip antenna on the radio box indicates that this department broadcasts on the 800 MHz band.

similar in coverage to that of a football helmet. Both the half-shell and three-quarter shell helmets have small visors. Full-face helmets offer the best possible protection for any motorcycle rider, but have never gained much acceptance by motor officers in the United States. Full-face helmets are used extensively by European motor officers. Although the full-face helmet offers the most protection, there are several disadvantages to police work. The officer's face is completely hidden from the person he may be speaking to. Not being able to clearly see an officer's face tends to make citizens feel uncomfortable. The officer's speech is often muffled by the full-face helmet, making it more difficult for the citizen to hear and understand what is being said. Police officers also report that the full-face helmet's restricted peripheral vision when off the motorcycle is a disadvantage that

far outweighs any benefit this helmet may provide in an accident. The two major manufacturers of helmets for police use are Bell and Shoei. The outer shells of these helmets are made of either fiberglass or a combination of Kevlar and fiberglass.

Air vents in the front of the helmet allow a small amount of air to circulate around the officer's head. But, for the most part, helmets are hot and may be uncomfortable. The sun beats down and creates a Crock-Pot™ effect inside. Some officers wear a small cotton helmet liner, but most leave their helmets on, even when off the bike for a short time, dealing with the heat as best they can. The other less serious disadvantage to wearing a helmet is the inevitable "helmet hair"—that coiffure of matted, squashed-down, pushed-out-of-shape thatch that is the result of wearing a close fitting helmet on a sweating head.

Cleanliness is a Family Affair

One of the benefits of being a motor officer is having a single motorcycle assigned to you as the exclusive rider; another is being able to ride your motorcycle to and from the station. Along with this "exclusive ownership" comes the responsibility of keeping the motorcycle white-glove clean. Most motor officers get additional pay for the time they spend at home keeping their motorcycles in spotless condition. Unlike show bikes, these workhorses are ridden in some of the most unlikely situations. Officers may have to take their motorcycles across fields of weeds and mud, chasing down a suspect. Even the daily road grime that accumulates from the highway needs to be removed. Cleaning a police motorcycle to showroom sparkle can take extraordinary measures.

In many instances, the motor officer's family is involved in the cleaning and detailing process. Jay Odom is a motor officer with the San Diego Police Department, where he rides a Kawasaki KZ1000. For the past two years, it's been the job of his son, Josh, to detail his motorcycle once a week. It usually takes three to four hours.

Motor officers are particularly picky when it comes to the appearance of their motorcycles. The cleaning and polishing of the officer's motorcycle is often entrusted to a family member. Here, Josh Odom is in the process of doing the weekly cleaning of his dad's Kawasaki.

He starts with the motorcycle out on the driveway, where he sprays the wheels and tires with cleaner. Then Josh mixes up a sudsy bucket full of a mild car-washing soap. He sprays down the bike with a hose, being careful not to get water on the instruments, lights, handlebar switches, or radio box. With a car washing mitt in hand, Josh scrubs down the bike. Following a quick rinse, his dad rolls the motorcycle into the garage so it won't water spot in the sun. Josh dries it with a cotton towel and uses compressed air to get water out of the nooks and crannies.

With the motorcycle clean and dry, Josh starts his polishing routine. He starts by spraying Armor All on the tires and wheels and lets it set while he waxes and polishes. Then Josh starts to wax the painted surfaces. He's found that Eagle One's Wet Look Paint Motorcycle Wax works best on the painted surfaces. On the chrome, Josh uses Mother's Chrome Polish. He doesn't use anything on the handgrips or seat surface, but a little Armor All is applied to the back of the seat. Once he's finished with the paint and chrome, Josh takes a rag and buffs off the wheels and tires. (When his dad drives his motorcycle to work following one of Josh's detail jobs, he rides very carefully for the first few miles until all the Armor All wears off the brake rotors and tire edges.) When he's finished, Josh puts the radar gun back in its holster, adds a fresh note pad to the handlebar clip, and hangs his dad's helmet on the mirror.

Does Josh do a good job? Without a doubt! Josh's dad is extremely picky about the appearance of his motorcycle and he's always pleased with the job his son does. Officer Odom also likes the praise he gets from his lieutenant whenever his motorcycle is inspected!

The red-and-blue forward-facing pursuit lights on this California Highway Patrol BMW are mounted high above each mirror. The square box on the engine guard is the siren speaker.

Leather Jacket

Part of the uniform that sets the motor officer
apart from the rest of the department is the leather
jacket. Motor officers just plain look cool wearing a
leather jacket, but wearing one of these jackets is part
tradition and part protection. The tradition dates
back to the earliest days, when police motorcycles
lacked the protection of a fairing or windshield.
Nearly every motor officer has a leather jacket, even
if it was not issued by his department. Leather jackets
worn by police motorcycle officers are not ordinary
off-the-rack models you might find at your local
motorcycle clothing dealer. Tabs on the front hold
the officer's badge, which must be displayed. Along
the bottom are retaining straps for the officer's duty
belt. The weight of the duty belt on the jacket keeps
the line of the jacket straight while the officer is on
the motorcycle. Some police leather jackets offer
hidden, protective panels inside that help prevent
injury in case of an accident.

Duty Belt

All motor officers must carry certain personal
safety items. For the most part, these items are carried on the duty belt, also called a gun belt or modi-

Spit-shined boots are part of the traditional motor officer's
uniform. These custom made boots can cost more than
$600 a pair and may last as long as three years. They are
replaced as soon as the stacks (the upper portion of the
boot that covers the calf) begin to fall, causing wrinkles at
the ankles. The top of the stack is a convenient place to
clip ballpoint pens.

For cold weather riding, nothing looks better than a motorcycle officer wearing a leather jacket. On the left side of the chest is a holder, where the officer has pinned his badge. On the right side is his name tag. Along the bottom edge of the jacket are retainers for the officer's duty belt. This spreads the weight of the belt over the jacket and keeps the jacket from rising up in the back when at speed. It also ensures that the items on the belt are easily accessible.

fied Sam Browne. Duty belts have traditionally been made of leather, but today they are also seen in nylon. Years ago, the only thing carried on the duty belt was the officer's weapon and spare ammunition. Today, the duty belt also carries numerous other items required for police work.

The days of the .38 Special police revolver are almost gone, since most officers who work the streets now carry a semiautomatic handgun. The most popular is a 9-millimeter, but 10-millimeter, .40-caliber, and .45-caliber weapons are also used. The larger calibers are becoming more popular to compete with the heavy-duty firearms often used by criminals on American streets. The holster used to carry a sidearm

is attached to the officer's duty belt. The standard holster holds the gun at waist level with the grip at, or slightly above, the belt level. Motor officers have the option of wearing a holster that hangs down lower on the hip. This holster has a swivel that ensures the gun is always pointing downward, even when the officer is seated on the motorcycle. All holsters have a retention strap to hold the gun securely in place. While no police officer ever hopes to use his gun, they all train to stay proficient in its use.

Also attached to the duty belt are cases to hold handcuffs, mace, a portable radio, and an extra magazine for the gun. The officer's baton is also attached to the belt by a simple ring attachment. Most

45

Each motor officer wears breeches while on duty. Breeches are tight fitting pants that are tucked into the top of the boots. They, like the boots, are a vestige of the days when officers rode horses.

These California Highway Patrol officers are wearing a helmet style known as a three-quarter shell. It's an open-face design that provides plenty of protection. Just above the gold braid are two small air vents that allow air to circulate inside. Both officers are wearing body armor under their uniform shirts. Also of note are the sunglasses and gloves rolled back one turn at the cuff.

departments require officers to carry these items. In addition, some officers will carry an extra magazine, an extra set of handcuffs, or a flashlight. Each additional item adds weight to a belt that is already heavy. Placement of each item on the duty belt is carefully calculated to suit each officer's personal preference and comfort. In the midst of a threatening situation, the officer must be able to pull another magazine from the belt without taking his eyes off of the action occurring around him. The same is true for the placement of handcuffs. When cuffing a suspect, the officer can't be fumbling for his handcuffs. They must be removed from the case and put to use in one fluid motion. Like the duty belt and holster, the equipment cases are either made of leather or nylon.

Whistles are still carried by officers in the traffic division and highway patrol. They are used to get the attention of drivers when working a traffic situation,

These CHP officers are wearing two different styles of jacket. The officer in the foreground has on a traditional leather jacket, and the other officer wears a cloth jacket. Both are wearing turtleneck sweaters.

This California highway patrol officer's motorcycle and uniform sparkle. His semiautomatic pistol is carried in a leather holster that has a basket weave pattern. Additional magazines for his gun and his traffic whistle are carried on his duty belt. Just barely visible behind the saddlebag is a nightstick.

When a motor officer turns on his emergency lights, he wants everyone to see him. This BMW is equipped with forward- and rear-facing red and blue strobes. It also has side-facing white strobes located on the bodywork, just above the engine's cylinders.

such as coordinating traffic at the end of a sporting event, at an accident scene, or when a traffic signal light fails. The whistle is a very simple solution to the problem of getting people to pay attention. Some officers carry personal pagers and cell phones to keep in contact with the outside world. One last item a motor officer carries is sun screen. Out in the elements for eight hours or more each day, a motor officer's arms and neck take a beating from the sun. For protection, many officers opt for long-sleeve shirts right through the summer months.

The final touches of a motor officer's uniform include gloves and sunglasses. Rarely will you ever see a motor officer without sun glasses. Most departments require that the lenses be shatter-proof plastic. Years ago, the aviator style was the most common. But today, the wraparound style is *de rigueur* for the younger officers. For night riding, many departments require their officers to wear clear glasses with shatterproof lenses.

Gloves are another important part of any motorcycle rider's attire. In a fall, gloves offer protection to the tender skin on the hands. While riding, gloves protect the hands from the chilling effect of the wind, abrasions from road grit, and bug strikes. For cold weather, motor officers wear a heavier, gauntlet-style glove. Summer wear is usually a thinner motorcycle glove or leather work glove. Another fashion quirk preserved from the old days is to turn up the glove's cuff one roll. Turning the cuff forward also gives the officer a better view of his or her wrist watch. It's part of the tradition and part of the police motorcycle cool.

The left-hand grip on this Harley-Davidson Road King houses the switch for the siren. When turned to the "on" position, it produces the wailing siren sound we are familiar with. The lever below is used to augment that wail with "whoops." *James Genat*

3

Training—
Getting Up on
Two Wheels

For those of you who have never ridden a motorcycle, it should be noted that unlike a car, riding a motorcycle is an active, rather than passive, affair. A car has four wheels for support, and the driver can easily drive with one hand, one foot, and often one eye. On a motorcycle, the rider needs both hands, both feet, and both eyes working in close concert with the brain. Losing concentration for a few seconds while driving a car may scare the driver a little, but on a motorcycle it could get the rider killed.

All modern motorcycles sold in America have standardized controls. On the right handlebar is the throttle. If the right handgrip is released, the throttle's spring tension will snap it to the closed position

A training day for these experienced motor officers includes a refresher course in maneuvering at low speed through cones. The red-shirted instructor is explaining what is expected in the next drill.

with the engine resuming its idle. The lever on the right handgrip operates the hydraulically actuated front disc brake, which all modern motorcycles use. The lever on the left side of the handlebar is the clutch. At the front of the right floorboard is a pedal (or peg on the BMW) that actuates the rear wheel brake. To properly brake a motorcycle, both the front and rear brakes must be used in harmony. The front brake is the most important, because of the motorcycle's forward weight transfer under braking. On the left floorboard is the shifter. Unlike civilian street motorcycles, the Harley-Davidson and Kawasaki police motorcycles have a much larger shift lever that is actuated by the heel of the officer's boot for up-shifts and by the toe for down-shifts. (The BMW has only a toe shift.) The shifter is sequential. Each click advances one gear, either up or down. Between first and second gear is the neutral detent.

Almost anyone can learn the basics of riding a motorcycle. Doing it well takes time, and riding as well as a law enforcement officer takes a lot of time. The average rider needs only to keep from running off the road or hitting something while enjoying the road. Law enforcement officers not only must stay out of trouble, but they have to be alert for any traffic violators. They must also be able to pursue violators safely at a high rate of speed. During a pursuit, the officer must communicate to the dispatcher a description of the vehicle and its location. It is a very difficult job.

It wasn't until the 1940s that formalized motorcycle training was instituted by police departments. Prior to that time, if you said you could ride a motorcycle, that was usually enough. The Los Angeles Police Department's two-week training program started with a week of vehicle code training, in which the officers learned the laws to be enforced. The second week was devoted to riding the motorcycle. The officers were taught to kick start the

This officer shows great form as he weaves at low speed through a tight pattern of cones. He's sitting squarely on the seat, looking where he wants to go. With his left hand, he's feeding in a small amount of clutch to keep his motorcycle under constant power through the turn.

motorcycle as fast as they could, get it in gear, and get going. Temperamental Harley-Davidson models were often hard to turn over, and many speeders were spared getting a ticket, while the frustrated officer kicked the beast's starter again and again. The early training programs often lacked comprehensive planning and usually focused on practical riding tips. Trainees often spun "doughnuts" around pylons on a dirt course. Abandoned airport runways were used for high-speed riding, and evasive maneuvers were taught as obstacles were thrown into their path. It's a wonder anyone survived.

The California Highway Patrol has always been a leader in the effective use of motorcycles for law enforcement work. In 1960 the CHP upgraded its motorcycle training to a two-part course, offering both basic and advanced training. Although the course was developed specifically for the CHP, its expertise has always been available to other agencies.

The red-shirted instructors at San Bernardino's EVOC are all experienced motor officers. They closely monitor the students as they go through their exercises.

Heads must be up all the time when driving through the cones. The officers are taught to look where they intend to go. Looking down at the ground is forbidden and if a student is caught doing so, the student is yelled at by the instructors.

Training days are physically and mentally stressful. This officer is surveying the course, concentrating on what he must do to successfully navigate the cone pattern ahead of him.

Today numerous training centers throughout the country specialize in motorcycle operation, as it relates to law enforcement. The Northwestern University Traffic Institute, in conjunction with Harley-Davidson, operates a National Motorcycle Academy, which offers one- and two-week courses. The California Highway Patrol offers its course to members of all agencies, as does the San Bernardino County Sheriff's Department, which has a state-of-the-art training facility in southern California. It has been found over and over again that proper training saves lives. Experience riding a motorcycle as a civilian does not mean that a person possesses the mental or physical skills necessary to safely operate a motorcycle for police work. Police motorcycles have a load factor much higher than a pleasure cruiser. The distribution of that load is also unusual, resulting in some unique handling characteristics. Safe operation at high speed and maneuverability at slow speeds require skills that remain undeveloped in the average civilian rider. The technology and capabilities of today's police motorcycle far exceeds the abilities of most riders.

To demonstrate high-speed braking, the instructor winds his Kawasaki up to 70 miles per hour. He then leans on the brakes, bringing his motorcycle to a smooth stop, using the proper braking techniques taught in the class. These techniques include using both brakes for maximum stopping power.

The high-speed apex drill tests the officer's skill at squeezing his motorcycle between two cones in a turn. Speeds approach 70 miles per hour in this follow-the-leader drill. The officers must keep a high visual horizon and drive smoothly. While doing this exercise, it's not unusual for the officer to drag the motorcycle's floorboards while leaning through the turn.

One of the first things taught to motorcycle officers is the correct way to mount and dismount the motorcycle. All police motorcycles have a side stand that extends to the left side of the machine. This stand is used when the motorcycle is parked. When on this stand, the motorcycle leans to the left. This means that when approaching the motorcycle the left side is lowest and the right side is the highest. Most of us get on or off a motorcycle from the left side (because it is lower), swinging the right leg over the back of the bike. However, motorcycle officers are taught to get on and off of the motorcycle from the right side. Mounting the motorcycle this way for the first time feels exceptionally awkward and uncomfortable, but there are some very good safety reasons for using this technique. When the officer makes a traffic stop, getting off on the right side of the motorcycle moves him away from the traffic flow.

If the officer were to lose his balance when dismounting to the left, he could fall into the traffic lane. Also, dismounting on the right prevents the bike from falling on the officer if the side stand fails. When getting on or off the motorcycle, the officer grips the front wheel's handbrake.

Potential motor officers learn some basic techniques at these training courses that make them better riders and give them the expertise to avoid or minimize potential accidents. Failure to learn specific techniques leads to the inevitable consequences. For example, failure to learn proper head and eye placement—forgetting to look where you want to go, instead of where you are—causes improper positioning and lack of control and will result in hitting objects. Failure to coordinate clutch and throttle (that is, finding the friction point) will result in lack of control, motor stalling, and dumping the bike, with damage and injury. Failure to master controlled braking will result in not slowing fast enough, locking one or both brakes, brake fade, collision, crash, and injury. Failure to keep both feet on the floorboards, rather than on the ground, will result in lack of control, foot injury, poor clutch and throttle control, and lack of confidence. You get the idea—there's a lot to know.

Studies have shown that approximately three-fourths of all motorcycle accidents involve a collision with another vehicle, usually a passenger car. The driver of the car either did not see the motorcycle before the collision, or did not see the motorcycle until it was too late to avoid a crash. The most frequent accident between car and motorcycle occurs when the motorcycle is proceeding straight and the approaching automobile makes a left turn in front of the oncoming motorcycle. Students are taught to ride as though they were completely invisible to all drivers.

In single-motorcycle accidents, rider error is the most common factor. In this type of accident, the rider approaches a curve with too much speed and runs wide off the road. The other most common factor in single-bike accidents is improper braking. Locking the front brake on a motorcycle is a guaranteed recipe for disaster. With the front wheel locked, the motorcycle may "high side," launching the rider over the handlebars or over the bike's side. Students are taught to immediately release the front brake lever if the wheel should lock. Rear wheel skids are more easily controlled and survivable than front wheel skids. Students are taught that when the rear wheel locks, they should

Training days are also an opportunity to calibrate motorcycle speedometers. A patrol car equipped with radar is used (the small white circle between the push bars is the radar's antenna). The officer makes several runs at the radar car at 10-mile-per-hour speed increments from 40 to 90 miles per hour. Following the pass, the officer in the car radios the motor officer his actual speed and a record is kept. The blur going past the car is a California Highway Patrol Kawasaki at 90 miles per hour.

At the scene of a shooting, things happen quickly. The officer responding must be ready to act upon arrival. Often this means the officer doesn't have time to remove his riding gloves. Motor officers must be comfortable shooting with their gloves on. Officers returning fire from behind the motorcycle while concentrating on the target have been known to shoot a hole through the windshield.

release the pedal pressure gently until the rear wheel starts to turn.

Police officers must develop above-average skills in two very different styles of riding—low speed and high speed. Low-speed skills are taught so police officers can safely maneuver around and through traffic on congested city streets or when approaching an accident scene on a jammed highway. High-speed skills are taught not so much to catch speeders as for the safety of the officer. In fact, many departments have policies that require their motorcycle officers to terminate a pursuit at a predetermined speed. By then, patrol cars or air units should be in place to take over the pursuit.

Low-speed drills are practiced using rubber cones. These drills teach balance and coordination, while simulating in-field turning maneuvers in tight areas. In these exercises, the student must smoothly

Motor officers must also know how to defend themselves in a shooting situation. In this live-fire training scenario, the motor officer is using his motorcycle as a shield as he returns fire. To add to the confusion, noise level, and tension of the training situation, the red-shirted instructor in the background is yelling and firing his gun.

If you look closely, you can see that the engine guards on this Harley-Davidson FXRP have been wrapped with duct tape. It's not unusual for an officer to take a spill during a low-speed drill. This officer wants to be sure his chrome stays in pristine condition.

Police Motorcycles in Pop Culture

Police motorcycles have been part of our culture since they first rolled down Main Street. But it wasn't until 1973 that a police officer on a motorcycle became a star. The cult classic film *Electra Glide in Blue* starred Robert Blake as a disillusioned Arizona motorcycle officer. Blake's short-in-stature character struggled to make sense of the random violence and height discrimination he was enduring. Blake rode a Harley-Davidson Electra Glide in the movie, and in the final scene, was shot and killed while trying to do a good deed.

Magnum Force was also released in 1973. It was one of the "Dirty Harry" films that starred Clint Eastwood as detective Harry Callahan. In this film, several young San Francisco motor officers decide to take the law into their own hands. These clean-cut officers (David Soul, Tim Matheson, and Robert Urich) go on a killing spree, indiscriminately knocking off bad guys. The motorcycles featured in *Magnum Force* were Moto Guzzis, a popular police motorcycle at the time.

The most popular television show featuring police motorcycles is the series *CHiPs*, which debuted in 1977 and still airs today in syndication. Erik Estrada as Ponch and Larry Wilcox as John did their best to look and act like California Highway Patrol officers while riding their Kawasakis. They were the first to bring the motor officer's romance of the road into American homes. Almost every show had a high-speed pursuit and at least one car that, when it ran into another vehicle, vaulted into the air, rolling and streaming flames. The vehicle's occupants were never severely hurt, even though they never wore their seat belts. If someone was trapped in their vehicle, the valiant heroes were always able to extricate the trapped souls just prior to the car or truck's gas tank exploding. Once clear of

The Speedvision cop is probably the most feared police motorcycle officer on the road. Not because of the tickets he writes, but because of his psychotic personality. © Speedvision

the burning vehicle, one of the two stars would invariably shout, "Stand back—it's going to blow!" Some of the early shows depicted real police work, but as the series progressed, the story lines degenerated, making for hilarious viewing today.

My personal police motorcycle television favorite is *The Andy Griffith Show*, Episode No. 112, titled "Barney's Sidecar." In this episode, the irrepressible Deputy Barney Fife buys a war surplus Harley-Davidson, complete with sidecar attached, and adds it to Mayberry's rolling stock. Deputy Fife then goes on a traffic enforcement rampage, writing citations for nine-elevens (illegal U-turn, five-dollar fine), one-fifteens (illegal parking, two-dollar fine), and just about everything else in the Mayberry vehicle code book. The good citizens of Mayberry are about to lynch Deputy Fife when Sheriff Taylor once again comes to Barney's rescue. The good sheriff plants a crude wooden sign, made by his son, Opie, under the seat of the sidecar. The sign indicates that this particular motorcycle had an important role in the liberation of Europe during World War II. With sign in hand, Andy convinces Barney that the motorcycle should be donated to the local VFW hall, where it will be put on permanent display. Barney, always wanting to do the right thing, relents and gives up his cherished motorcycle.

Today, the most visible and originally funny police motorcycle officer does 30-second spots for the Speedvision cable television network. He rides a Harley-Davidson Electra Glide and terrorizes motorists on a stretch of Southwest desert highway. Along the road, he stops Craig Breedlove in a rocket car, menaces the owner of a 1957 Corvette for using duct tape to repair a seat, and humiliates the owners of an AMC Gremlin, ridiculing their poor transportation choice.

Slow right-hand turns are the hardest to execute on a motorcycle, because the rider's clutch control arm (left) is fully extended, making it difficult to make the necessary minute corrections to the clutch.

execute the throttle and clutch control, and maintain overall balance. The student's feet should never touch the ground; they should always be planted firmly on the floorboards. Low-speed drills are done on both level and inclined surfaces. The students must learn to properly apply rear brake only when on the down side of the incline. Certain cone patterns are designed to require lock-to-lock turns. Handling a large motorcycle in tight spaces takes a high degree of skill, and these low-speed drills are designed to inspire confidence in the rider.

Countersteering is a unique phenomenon. It adds a high degree of maneuverability to a motorcycle at speed. Upon trying it for the first time, one student claimed it was like adding power steering to the motorcycle. Countersteering goes against the logic of the brain. The student is told to push on the motorcycle's left handgrip to go left and the right handgrip to go right, effectively turning the motorcycle's front wheel in the opposite direction of the turn. The dynamics of countersteering set the motorcycle into a lean, exactly the attitude it should have in a high-speed turn. Countersteering is a defensive tactic that teaches methods other than braking to avoid accidents. Countersteering drills are set up on the high-speed section of the course, where the students must pass through a small opening between two cones at a high rate of speed. This exercise also teaches the students to maintain a high visual horizon and to keep head and eyes up. Students are taught that if they apply their brakes while in a curve, the motorcycle will want to straighten up and go wide.

Motor officers who have taken specialized motorcycle training courses come away having learned things that may one day save their lives or minimize injury. Even veteran officers who have ridden motorcycles for years benefit from new training techniques. At one time, officers were taught to lay the bike down in anticipation of a crash. Today, they are taught about the benefits of dual braking, to

A motor officer's attitude and degree of skill are the two primary factors in safe motorcycle operation. Studies have shown that refresher training for the experienced officer lowers accident rates.

bleed off as much speed as possible prior to a collision. Understanding the physical characteristics of bodies in motion leads to safer riding.

In all courses designed for motor officers, students experience an intense level of competition and a drive to excel. Often as a matter of personal pride, students will spend extra time drilling with fellow officers. Body aches, pains, and cramps in the areas of the neck, shoulders, arms, and hands are not unusual, nor is a high level of frustration in learning these new skills.

Grading and evaluation standards ensure that those who pass are fully qualified in all areas of motorcycle handling and safety. Those who do not pass are either not motorcycle officer material, or they have not quite mastered the necessary skills to ride safely as a law enforcement officer. No favoritism is extended to nice guys. An officer is either qualified and safe, or the recommendation is made to the officer and his or her department that the officer shouldn't be riding a motorcycle.

using the motorcycle as a shield. The officer is to empty two magazines at the suspects. To add a sense of realism to the scenario, the instructor yells and fires rounds in the background. This is done to simulate the confusion and noise at the scene of a shooting. It's not unusual for an officer to accidentally shoot a hole in the windshield of his motorcycle.

Like police officers who work out of a patrol car, motorcycle officers must be prepared for the worst whenever they make a traffic stop. A simple technique is used to get off the bike quickly and be prepared for the unknown. Once the motorcycle has come to a complete stop, the officer drops the kick stand with his or her left foot, while simultaneously turning the engine switch to off with his or her right hand. This is done as the officer keeps his or her eyes on the suspect in the car he or she has just stopped. The officer shifts his or her weight to the right, and puts his or her right foot on the ground. While the officer is doing this, the right hand is on the holster, and the left hand comes across and grabs the right handgrip. As the officer swings off the bike on the right side, he or she is firmly balanced with the left hand on the right handgrip and the right foot on the ground. During all of this, the officer's eyes have never left the suspect in the car, and his or her hand is still on the holster. If something should happen, the officer is ready.

Training is an ongoing process. Each department sets regular training days, usually quarterly, for its motor officers. At each of these training days, a specific skill is refreshed, and the motorcycle speedometers are calibrated. For officers who spend most of their time on the highway, a low-speed cone pattern may be used to renew their traffic handling skills. Officers whose beats are mostly in the city may need high-speed cornering exercises. Large departments that escort motorcades regularly will include this as part of their education regime. Training brings new motor officers up to speed and sharpens the skills of even veteran motor officers.

One of the skills a motor officer acquires is defending against an armed suspect. Motor officers are taught to return fire, using their motorcycles as shields. This training, which takes place on a department range, is more difficult than at first may be imagined. Prior to the exercise, the training officer explains to the students what will happen and what is expected. Two outline targets, representing a driver and a passenger from a car that has been stopped for a traffic violation, are set up. The motor officer is to pull up, make a radio call for shots fired, dismount, and return fire,

4

On Patrol—
Sentinels of
the Streets

Being a motor officer is as much a lifestyle as it is a job. This lifestyle includes the uniform and a mode of transportation, in this case, the motorcycle. Most departments assign each officer his or her own personal motorcycle to ride both on patrol and to and from work. The police motor officers' duties are a little more sharply focused than those of their patrol officer counterparts. The motor

Because of their maneuverability, police motorcycles are often the first emergency vehicles to reach the scene of an auto accident. Once on scene, the officer quickly assesses victim injuries and calls for ambulances and tow trucks. Another responsibility of the motor officer at an accident scene is to direct traffic so emergency workers can do their work safely.

Motor officers enforce the traffic laws, and to do that, they must write tickets. This officer has his ticket book in hand and is filling in the pertinent data from the offender's registration and license.

officer is attached to the traffic division and almost exclusively attends to vehicle code infractions. Regular patrol officers handle a wide range of calls, which may also include traffic.

Most motor officers work the day shift, but not all departments restrict their motor units from riding at night. Riding during the hours of darkness is strictly a safety issue, for which each department has its own policy. Riding at night presents an entirely new set of challenges to the motor officer. It can be very difficult to see the road when riding a motorcycle at night. The motorcycle's single headlight has a limited range and illumination. Motorcycles are also more vulnerable to obstructions in the road at night. This problem, combined with limited lighting, makes for a dangerous situation. There are some motor officers who prefer the night shift and the cover it gives them when spotting violators. These offi-

cers have learned to effectively use the lights of other vehicles to augment their motorcycle's lights.

A Day in the Life

Most motor officers are assigned a motorcycle that they take home each day. Each work day starts with the ride to work. On the way to the station a motor officer is not officially on duty, but he or she may still make traffic stops. Once in the station, all officers sit through a line-up or briefing, which is where they are officially checked in by their sergeant. At this daily meeting, the sergeant will discuss any specific situations that could affect them on their shift. This might include road closures, a sporting event, a specific traffic problem area, or a new department policy. These meetings usually last less than half an hour.

This motor officer has stopped to chat with a fellow officer from the traffic division. Traffic division officers (in patrol cars or on motorcycles) are responsible for enforcing the vehicle code, for accident investigation, and for all other matters related to vehicle code enforcement. *James J. Genat*

Following line-up, the officers grab a quick cup of coffee before hitting the road. During this time, they will get together with other officers who cover the same area to discuss specific traffic problems. One officer may know of an intersection where people continually make illegal turns; another may have a problem with drivers ignoring the flashing red safety lights on school buses, or there may be a stretch of road where the speed limit is ignored. These officers may decide to pair up to cover the situation. Just as important will be their visibility in the area, which is a clear signal to the drivers that the traffic laws are being enforced. Many situations are governed by time of day and traffic flow. Once the officers feel that they have made an impact in the problem area, they will split up and cover specific beats.

Motor officers share a solid bond with each other. Usually, several will meet for lunch, discuss what their morning was like and share anything unusual. If there is another specific traffic problem brewing, the officers may team up to work it.

Finding traffic violators is as easy as shooting fish in a barrel—they're everywhere. Many people just don't obey traffic laws, and today's driver is in a big hurry. While speeding down the highway, some drivers eat a meal, others put on makeup, shave, talk on the phone, or even read the newspaper. Multiple distractions and the pressures of life are taken out on the road. Also, from a motorcycle it's very easy to see

Anyone who has ever ridden a motorcycle knows the thrill of entering a freeway on-ramp while rolling on the power and leaning into the turn. It's not unusual for police officers to lean their motorcycles over far enough to drag the bottom of the floor-boards on the pavement.

inside a car. Many officers have been able to spot open bottles of alcohol, drugs, and the punched-out ignition cylinder of a stolen car while they were riding alongside. In fact, many routine traffic stops lead to arrests for more serious offenses.

Most modern police cars have Mobile Data Terminals (MDTs) that allow the officer to

This California Highway Patrol officer has just finished making a traffic stop and is starting to roll into the traffic lane. The metal box in front of the saddlebag is where he keeps his ticket book.

communicate with a dispatcher electronically and retrieve all types of police records. Motorcycles are restricted to voice communications only. Each police vehicle is given a number to use when communicating with the dispatcher. Because of the number of traffic stops motorcycle units make on an average day, they may only contact the dispatcher when dealing with something fairly serious, like a possible stolen car or drunken driver. When a motor officer spots a car driving erratically and suspects a drunken driver, a typical call may go like this:

"Six-Twelve Mary, I'm stopping yellow Oldsmobile, California 3 Union King Edward 168, possible deuce, 1900 block Azure Way." Communication with the dispatcher always starts with the unit's call sign, in this case it is 6-12 Mary. This alerts the dispatcher that unit 6-12M is calling. What the officer then said, using police radio shorthand, was that he was stopping a yellow Oldsmobile, with California license plate 3UKE168. A "deuce" (referring to California Standard Code 502) is common California police slang for a drunken driver, and the stop is being made in the 1900 block of Azure Way. The dispatcher would then respond with "Six-Twelve Mary, 10-4." This confirms to the calling officer that the call has been received. The dispatcher would then enter the information into the computer. Also, all radio transmissions are tape recorded. This is done for various legal reasons, and for the opportunity to replay a call if the dispatcher is unsure of the communication.

At the scene, the officer makes contact with the driver of the car and finds that the female driver is not drunk, but was driving erratically because she was distraught over a disagreement with her boyfriend, and had been the victim of an assault. The officer notices that along with being visibly agitated, she is bruised, bleeding, and has an apparent broken finger. The officer then calls to the dispatcher, "Six Twelve Mary, deuce checks negative, I need

Motor officers will often team up to work a specific traffic enforcement problem. When riding in pairs, the officer on the left is the lead.

a patrol unit for possible DV 11-10 and 11-41 for one with head injuries, lacerations, and possible broken finger." The officer is letting the dispatcher know that the possible drunken driver situation he called in earlier is no longer valid. He then requests that a patrol car meet him at the scene to take a report (11-10). A request is made for an ambulance (11-41) for one person, and then the officer gives a brief description of the victim's injuries. The dispatcher would contact a patrol car in the area and give that officer the location and reason for the call. They would also contact an ambulance with information on the victim and the location.

Following the call to the dispatcher, the motor officer would let the victim know that an ambulance is on the way. Then he will ask the victim for a location and description of the boyfriend. That information (along with any knowledge of weapons in the suspect's possession) is given to the dispatcher and another patrol car is routed to detain the suspect until more information is obtained. Once the patrol unit arrives on the scene, the motor officer turns the incident over to them. The motor officer then calls the dispatcher and says "Six-Twelve-Mary, Clear Ten-Eight with a K." "Clear" means that the officer is finished with that stop, "Ten-Eight" means he's back in service and "with a K" means that there was no violation written by the motor officer, who is now back on patrol.

At the end of the day, the motor officers meet back at the station for another line-up. This is where they officially end their shift. It's at this time that each motor officer will catch up on the daily paperwork he or she must do. Following line-up, the officers get on their bikes and ride home.

The Motorcade

One of the most exciting events a motor officer can participate in is the motorcade escort. A motorcade is a car or group of cars escorted by a group of police motorcycles. It is used to provide secure, quick transit for a foreign visitor or American VIP who may need extra security or whose presence could cause a traffic jam. During the transit of the motorcade, regular traffic along the route and on cross streets is temporarily halted to allow safe movement for the visiting dignitary. The type of motorcade with which people are most familiar is the one used to transport the president of the United States. Motorcades are usually used for visiting heads of state, as well as the U.S. vice president. During an election year, the major candidates are also offered a police escort. Motorcades are also available to former U.S. presidents, but they generally favor a much more low-key method of transportation. Motorcades are also used for police and fire department funerals, special sporting events, such as the Indianapolis 500 and World Series, and other special events approved by the local chief of police.

Motorcades are planned far in advance of the actual event. If the president plans to visit a city on a certain date, the Secret Service contacts the local police department's intelligence unit. A meeting is arranged between those two groups and a motor sergeant from the traffic department. The motor sergeant is responsible for arranging a safe transit route along the host city's roads. Once the sergeant has planned the motorcade route, the sergeant presents it to the Secret Service agent-in-charge and to the representative from his or her local intelligence department. Weeks prior to the arrival, all three will drive or fly along the route in a department helicopter. Generally, the routes for a presidential visit are defined by a few known locations—the airport where *Air Force One* will land, the hotel where the president is staying, and the location of the event he is attending. The route connecting those locations will be the most direct. Occasionally, the dignitary will make a special request, such as the time Russian leader Mikhail Gorbachev wanted to stop at the Hard Rock Cafe in Chicago for a beer. It wasn't on the schedule, but the motor officers accommodated his request.

On the day of the motorcade, the sergeant in charge will assemble his or her team of officers. For a presidential motorcade, the officer may need as many as 20 motor officers; for a sports bus, it may require only 6. A route card is given to each officer. This card details the beginning of the motorcade and its final destination. The route is broken down into several "points," which may be an intersection of two

This motor officer is using a laser gun to monitor speed on a residential street. Because of the laser's long range, he can track a speeding car from more than 2,000 feet away. Once he's gotten a reading on a violator, he will step out into the street and flag over the driver. And when a scowling motor officer points at you—you pull over.

roads or a highway entrance or exit ramp. The point references are used as radio shorthand because it's much easier to say "passing point one" than "passing the intersection of Harper Ranch Road and East Warmlands Avenue." This is especially true if one or both of these streets is crossed more than once during the duration of the motorcade. This radio shorthand also works as a code known only to those with a route card. If someone were to scan the radio frequency the motor officers were using, they would have no idea of the motorcade's location.

The group of vehicles to be escorted in a motorcade is called the "secure package." A marked police car acts as the lead car, and another marked police unit follows at the end. The cars in between include the dignitary's limousine, a back-up limo, and cars carrying personal security staff and other VIPs. As the motorcade proceeds, the lead and tail police cars will have their light bars activated, but not their sirens. All police officers in the motorcade communicate using one of the local department's tactical radio frequencies. This gives the motorcade its own radio channel. The department's standard radio frequency is left open for regular police business. Because of the verbal shorthand of the point system, radio chatter is kept to a minimum.

The sergeant who planned the route will be the "pilot" motorcycle. His or her position will be 600 to 1,000 feet in front of the motorcade. The sergeant is in complete control of the group's movement, but he

These motor officers have stopped a suspected armed felon and are in the process of removing him from the car. They are crouching behind their motorcycles with their guns drawn. The suspect has been ordered to place his hands out the open window. *James J. Genat*

Once out of the car, the suspect reaches for the sky. He is ordered to walk backward to the officers' position and then to kneel on the ground. The officers stay crouched behind their Harley-Davidson motorcycles until they're sure they are safe. *James J. Genat*

The officer on the left is about to handcuff the kneeling subject. The officer on the right is still behind his motorcycle, watching his partner and keeping an eye on the car in case someone else is hidden inside. At the onset of this stop, a radio call would have been placed to the dispatcher for assistance from other patrol units in the area. *James J. Genat*

77

One occasion for which motor officers turn out *en mass* is for the funeral of a firefighter or police officer. These officers not only pay their respects but control traffic for the large motorcade. *Dale Stockton*

or she may have another motor officer riding a short distance behind. That motor officer's role is to cover any vehicle or intersection that may have been overlooked by the others. Directions for this officer are given directly by the sergeant-in-charge. At the rear is another motor sergeant. It is this sergeant's responsibility to control traffic, civilian cars, and police motorcycles that may follow the motorcade.

There are two methods of conducting a motorcade. In the first, each motor officer is given one or more specific locations to cover, known as "posts." A post may be a highway entrance ramp or a surface street intersection. The motor officer positions himself or herself at the first location, and, after the motorcade passes, heads out for the next assigned post. This is a good method, except it offers little or no backup in case an officer cannot make the assigned post. A delay may be caused by a mechanical malfunction of the motorcycle or by an accident needing immediate attention.

With the second method, called the "rolling closure," motorcycles are used much more effectively. As the motorcade is about to depart, the lead sergeant dispatches the officers to the road. Looking at their route cards, they disperse themselves along the beginning of the route. The first officers out will take the first posts along the route, and as others proceed they will pass by the officers who have already posted. When coming upon the next open post, the

motor officer will stop and hold position. As the motorcade passes, the posted officer will climb on his or her motorcycle and fall in behind the end of the motorcade. When safe, the officer will pass the motorcade and search for the next open post along the route. This system offers a great deal of flexibility and all posts can be covered by a number of different officers.

The rolling closure also frees officers to investigate and handle anything out of the ordinary. For instance, if there were a vehicle broken down along the route, an officer would stop, investigate, and stay with that vehicle until the motorcade had passed. If there was a problem that could endanger the motorcade, the officer contacts the lead sergeant and appropriate action is taken. This might include taking an alternate route. An officer who stops along the

route will keep his back to the motorcade and his eyes on his posted point until the motorcade passes. It's that officer's job to watch stopped cars for any suspicious activity until the "secure package" has passed. Most of the time, the officer will dismount the motorcycle. This gives drivers a better view of the officer, and the officer a better view of each driver.

When the motorcade must travel along a multi-lane freeway, traffic on the road must be stopped to allow the motorcade to enter. This is done by creating a traffic break. Several officers join the flow of traffic at approximately one mile before the motorcade's entrance. They activate their rear emergency lights and start to weave across the lanes of traffic. Once they have all the lanes covered, they will slow down and finally stop before reaching the ramp that the motorcade will be using. Traffic in front of the

This is what it looks like from the driver's seat of a Kawasaki KZ1000 police motorcycle at speed.

Police Bicycles

Most police officers who ride bicycles say the city of Seattle is the birthplace of the modern bicycle officer. Putting police officers on bicycles is a simple concept that has proven to be extremely effective in patrolling congested downtown and beach areas. Police bicycles are highly mobile, and they can be quite stealthy.

The big advantage for officers on police bicycles is the face-to-face access to citizens in the community. Bicycle officers are highly visible and approachable. Police departments have found that people are more willing to stop and converse with an officer on a bike than one in a patrol car. With this type of community policing, residents have a better rapport with police. Another advantage of a police bicycle is that it can navigate areas a patrol car or police motorcycle can't, such as the sidewalks of apartment complexes, car ports, and small alleyways.

The machine of choice for bicycle patrol units is the mountain bike. They are sturdy machines with multiple speeds that allow officers to comfortably ride on virtually any surface. The price for the basic bike can range as high as $1,000 for one with an aluminum frame and suspended front fork. Storage bags for the necessities of law enforcement are available for the crossbar or over the rear wheel as saddlebags. A wide variety of battery-powered lights is also available for police work,

Like many big cities, Fort Worth, Texas, has instituted police bike patrols. Officers selected for this type of work use mountain bikes and receive special training in how to effectively use the bike for law enforcement. *Dale Stockton*

including red and blue strobes and sirens.

Like motor officers, bicycle officers volunteer for this duty. Each officer attends an intensive, one-week course on how to most effectively use the bicycle on patrol. Officers are taught about proper nutrition and keeping properly hydrated. Tactics are taught in how to conduct a vehicle stop, chase a subject, ride up and down steps, and how to use the bike as a form of protection. They are taught how to use the speed and stealth of a bike to capture suspects. One stealth technique used is called "soft pedaling," which involves rotating the pedals slowly while coasting. This technique eliminates the clicking in the rear wheel hub. Officers are also taught to dismount while still rolling. The rider swings the right leg over and coasts to a stop, the left foot still on the left pedal. As the bike comes to a stop, the right foot pulls down the kick stand. The officer is now free of the bike and ready to go.

Like motor officers, bicycle officers have their own unique uniform. Because the officers are out in the warm weather months, clothes that keep them cool are a necessity. Nylon bike shorts and polo shirts are most typically worn, topped off with a bicycle helmet. On an average shift, a bicycle patrol an officer can ride as many as 20 miles. And as you can imagine, the bicycle officers are some of the fittest officers on the force.

Once a year in the city of San Bernardino, California, the officers get to adorn their motorcycles with flames for the Route 66 Rendezvous. This annual muscle car and hot rod street party draws 3,000 participants and more than 250,000 spectators. The city's motor officers are highly visible during the event, cruising the same route along with the hot-rodders.

officers will continue along the road at its normal speed, thereby leaving an empty, open stretch of road for the motorcade. Once it has passed, the officers quickly join up on the tail end and then pass the motorcade on their way to the next post. The traffic that was halted can now move ahead, but is not allowed to pass the motorcade. It's the job of the sergeant at the rear of the motorcade to keep watch over the traffic behind him or her and not allow any vehicles, other than police motorcycles, to pass.

Typically, a motorcade travels in the right-hand lane of a road. Police motorcycles passing en route to the next post do so on the left for safety. If the road narrows to one lane or if an entrance or exit ramp lies ahead, the lead sergeant makes the call "32 Sam, do not pass," (32 Sam is the call sign for the lead sergeant) which informs the motor officers in the rear to stand by. Once the road opens up for passing, the lead sergeant makes the call that it's clear to pass. Motorcade speeds are kept to a maximum of 55 miles per hour. This gives the motor officers enough time to accelerate and pass the motorcade.

As the sergeant in the lead passes each predetermined route point, he or she calls them out on the

Criminals drive cars—it's an axiom that all motor officers know well. While making routine traffic stops, many officers have happened upon wanted felons. In this traffic stop, the driver receives only a citation. *Dale Stockton*

Following a motorcade, the participating officers smartly line up their motorcycles. Once they dismount, the officers will stand at parade rest in front of their motorcycles. It's customary for the dignitary being escorted to come over and shake each officer's hand in appreciation.

Motorcycle officers make a lot of traffic stops during the course of their day. Most officers call in to the dispatcher only when they feel the person being stopped may present a problem.

radio to let the other officers know the exact location of the motorcade. At the final destination, the motor officers line up their motorcycles and stand in front of them smartly. More often than not, the dignitary will come over and shake hands with the officers.

In 1996, the Republican National Convention took place in San Diego, California. It was the responsibility of the San Diego Police Department to coordinate the motorcades for the Republican presidential candidate, Bob Dole, and for the vice presidential candidate, Jack Kemp. Veteran San Diego motor officer Jay Odom was one of the motor officers assigned to Jack Kemp. "A majority of the officers were assigned to Bob Dole," recollects Odom. "But there were 10 of us and a couple of

Right
Catching traffic violators is sometimes as easy as shooting fish in a barrel. This motor officer is running his hand-held radar on the cars coming down the hill. On this particular day, he was stopping only those drivers who exceeded the posted speed limit (35 miles per hour) by 15 miles per hour.

Previous Page
Throughout an officer's law enforcement career, he makes many friends in all areas of law enforcement. This motor sergeant has stopped by the department's air unit to chat with one of the pilots. While parked, he's hung his helmet on the motorcycle's mirror, a common place for a motor officer to hang his hat. The helicopter is a Bell Jetranger. The dark circular object under its belly is the FLIR (Forward Looking Infrared).

supervisors assigned to escort Kemp around. He went a lot of places, so we were always on the go." It was a solid week of motorcades for the SDPD. Four would often be going at the same time—one each for the two candidates and two minimotorcades for the candidate's wives. Planning was done quickly and efficiently with the help of the department's Criminal Intelligence Unit. "We'd have a short meeting with the motor sergeants and the detectives who were running it," Odom said. "They'd say, 'We're going from here to there, and this is the way we want to travel.' So we'd go!" Often Kemp's motorcade had to slow its arrival in order to follow Dole's motorcade at certain locations. "Kemp stayed out later at night and went to more parties than Bob Dole did—so we put in some overtime. You'd have several hours of down time, but then you were just on an adrenaline rush

Code Two is a quick response by a police motorcycle to a situation with no lights or siren. Code Three is a rapid response with lights and siren.

Following a freeway accident, two CHP motor officers and one patrol officer discuss how they are going to handle the preliminary investigation. A description of the scene and measurements of skid marks are taken down in notepads.

Motorcycles tend to go where the rider is looking, and this officer is looking through the turn to the road ahead. The shifting of his body weight on the machine is making the motorcycle turn.

For a motor officer, one of the keys to catching a speeder is quick acceleration. The officer must attain a speed at least 20 miles per hour faster than the violator in order to reach the violator in a reasonable amount of time. Many departments have policies that restrict high-speed pursuits beyond predetermined speeds.

that you wouldn't believe. That was the most fun I've ever had on motors. I loved it!"

The great advantage to being a police motor officer is the independence the motorcycle allows. Motor officers are self-starters; in fact, having initiative was one of the things that got them on motors to begin with. Motor officers don't need a lot of direction. Their attitude is, "Just tell me what you want me to do, and I'll go out and do it." Because of the independent, self-initiated nature of these men and women, they generally ride alone. If, while riding in a pair, one officer were to make a traffic stop, the other officer would be required to stand idly by until his or her partner finished. There are occasions, however, when officers are seen riding together. If one of the officers is assigned to a problem area and needs some assistance in effective enforcement, then the officers will travel together to that location.

San Diego Police Department motor officer Chuck Shipler is not fond of riding in pairs. "The reason a lot of officers don't like riding in pairs is that a little bit of their attention must be on the other rider in close proximity." Riding in pairs takes a lot of concentration because the officers like to keep close together. It takes skill and it also looks good. "What we do, we try to do well. That's why we're on motors," says Shipler. "When riding with another officer, I don't get as much activity. I'm not looking as hard, because I'm paying more attention to the person I'm with."

Motor officers, whether in a group or individually, prefer to ride in the left lane. It's the lane most frequently free of debris and road hazards. And all good motorcycle riders, police or civilian, avoid the grease strip that runs down the center of each traffic lane.

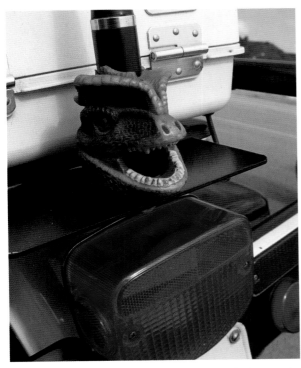

Often, you have to look closely to find the little ways in which motor officers personalize their motorcycles. Stuck on the radio's antenna, this rubber dragon's head grins eerily at all those who follow this motor officer.

One situation where a pair of motor officers is a distinct advantage is at an accident scene, especially if the accident happens on a congested highway. Because of their maneuverability, police motorcycles can often be the first to reach a highway accident. With two officers on the scene, one can help the victims and the other can work traffic.

Riding motorcycles all day and getting paid for it is a lifestyle that's hard to give up. Many officers have passed up promotions that would have taken them off the motorcycle. Motor officers love what they do—and they do it well.

When pursuing a speeder on a highway, the motor officer first activates the lights on the rear of the motorcycle, alerting the traffic to the rear to stay back. Once the officer has closed in on the offending vehicle, he will pace him for a few seconds to confirm the speed violation. As soon as the speed reading has been confirmed, the officer will activate his forward-facing emergency lights. If the driver does not respond, the officer will give a quick blast of the siren. Sirens are less effective on the freeway than in the city, because of the large open area surrounding the road and the ambient noise created by the vehicle speed.

Index